W9-BNT-684
11/15

FREAKY FREELOADERS

BUGS THAT FEED ON PEOPLE

CODY KEISER

New York

FREMONT PUBLIC LIBRARY DISTRICT
1170 N. Midlothian Road
Mundelein, IL 60060
WITHDRAWN

Published in 2016 by The Rosen Publishing Group, Inc.
29 East 21st Street, New York, NY 10010

Copyright © 2016 by The Rosen Publishing Group, Inc.

All rights reserved. No part of this book may be reproduced in any form without permission in writing from the publisher, except by a reviewer.

First Edition

Editor: Katie Kawa
Book Design: Michael J. Flynn

Photo Credits: Cover, p. 1 (flea) Robert Pickett/Visuals Unlimited/Getty Images; cover, pp. 3–24 (frame) Dinga/Shutterstock.com; pp. 4, 6, 7 (cat flea), 10, 12, 16, 18 (fleas) Wim van Egmond/Visuals Unlimited/Getty Images; pp. 5, 11 (adult) smuay/Shutterstock.com; p. 7 (dog flea) http://en.wikipedia.org/wiki/Dog_flea#mediaviewer/File:Ctenocephalides-canis.jpg; p. 7 (human flea) Cosmin Manci/Shutterstock.com; p. 7 (Oriental rat flea) Photo Researchers/Science Source/Getty Images; p. 8 iStock/Thinkstock.com; pp. 9, 11 (pupa) Bianca Lavies/National Geographic/Getty Images; p. 11 (eggs) Agency-Animal-Picture/Getty Images; p. 11 (larva) http://en.wikipedia.org/wiki/Flea#mediaviewer/File:Flea_Larva.jpg; p. 13 (cat hair) schankz/Shutterstock.com; pp. 13 (flea), 15 Daniel Cooper/E+/Getty Images; p. 14 FCG/Shutterstock.com; p. 17 DEA/G. DAGLI ORTI/De Agostini Picture Library/Getty Images; p. 19 (rat) Liukov/Shutterstock.com; p. 19 (flea) http://commons.wikimedia.org/wiki/File:Xenopsylla_cheopis_flea_PHIL_2069_lores.jpg; p. 20 Charles Mann/E+/Getty Images; p. 21 Michal Ludwiczak/Shutterstock.com; p. 22 Carolina K. Smith MD/Shutterstock.com.

Library of Congress Cataloging-in-Publication Data

Keiser, Cody.
Fleas / by Cody Keiser.
p. cm. — (Freaky freeloaders: bugs that feed on people)
Includes index.
ISBN 978-1-4994-0750-1 (pbk.)
ISBN 978-1-4994-0752-5 (6 pack)
ISBN 978-1-4994-0753-2 (library binding)
1. Fleas — Juvenile literature. I. Title.
QL599.5 K457 2016
595.77'5—d23

Manufactured in the United States of America

CPSIA Compliance Information: Batch #WS15PK: For Further Information contact Rosen Publishing, New York, New York at 1-800-237-9932

CONTENTS

FREAKY FLEAS

People often think of fleas as tiny bugs that live on dogs and cats. However, they can live on many other animals, too, such as birds, foxes, and rats. Fleas can even live on people!

Fleas live on the bodies of people and other animals because they drink blood. They're part of a group of living things called parasites. Parasites feed on the bodies of other animals, which are called hosts. Some parasites can make their hosts very sick.

Fleas bite hosts to feed on their blood. Some fleas spread deadly sicknesses by biting sick animals and then biting healthy people.

SO MANY SPECIES!

Different kinds of fleas feed on different kinds of animals. There are around 2,000 different species, or kinds, of fleas in the world. Some of the most common fleas that feed on human blood are cat fleas, dog fleas, and human fleas. However, human fleas aren't often found in North America.

Cat fleas are found on humans more often than dog fleas. Cat fleas live on both dogs and cats, too, as well as foxes, leopards, and many other **mammals**.

FREAKY FACT!

FLEAS FEED ON MANY ANIMALS. HOWEVER, SOME OF THE ANIMALS THEY AREN'T KNOWN TO FEED ON INCLUDE APES, MONKEYS, AND HORSES.

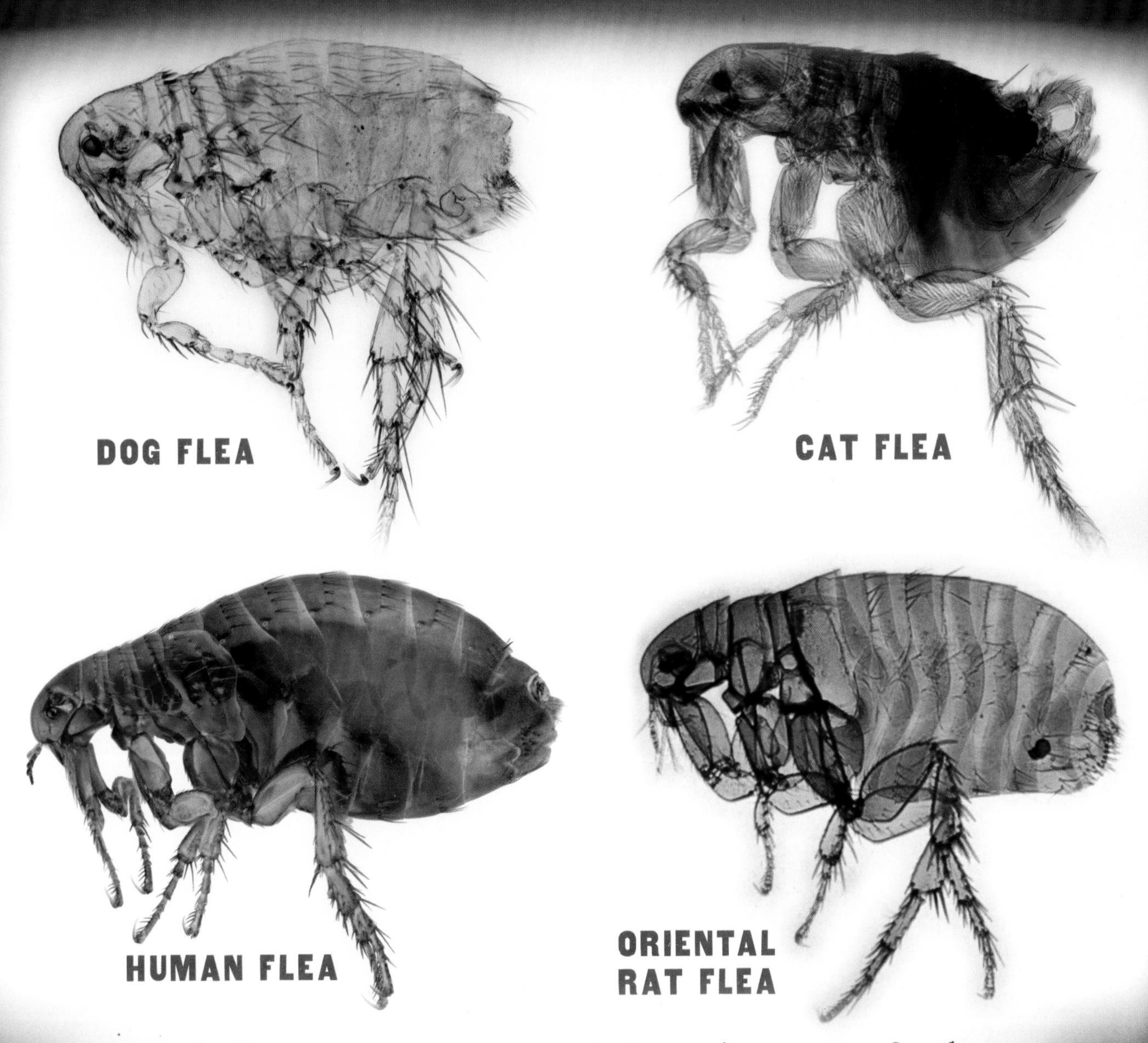

These flea species have all been known to feed on human blood. The Oriental rat flea can spread a very deadly sickness, called bubonic plague, to people.

A CLOSER LOOK

Fleas are often hard to see on the bodies of their hosts because they're so small. They're between 0.039 and 0.39 inch (0.1 and 1 cm) long. Fleas have a flat, reddish-brown body. Their flat body allows them to move easily between a host's hairs or feathers.

A flea's body is covered in **spines**. These spines help the flea hold on tightly to the host's body, even when its hair or fur is being combed.

FLEA SPINES

A flea's body has special **adaptations** to help it stay on its host, so it can get plenty of food.

FROM EGG TO ADULT

Fleas can be found around people's homes in every **stage** of their life cycle. A life cycle is a set of stages a living thing goes through from the time it's born until the time it dies. A flea's life cycle has four stages.

A flea starts its life as an egg. Then, it grows into a wormlike larva. A flea larva then spins a cocoon around itself and enters the pupa stage. After it comes out of its cocoon, it's an adult flea.

FREAKY FACT!

FLEA LARVAE EAT THE WASTE THAT COMES OUT OF AN ADULT FLEA'S BODY IN ORDER TO FEED ON BLOOD THAT'S ALREADY BEEN EATEN. THEY ALSO EAT BITS OF DEAD SKIN AND FEATHERS FROM HOST ANIMALS.

LIFE CYCLE OF A FLEA

EGG

- white oval
- laid on the body or in the living space of host animal

LARVA

- looks like a worm
- legless and blind

ADULT

- can live for a few weeks to over a year, depending on species
- lays eggs to start a new life cycle

PUPA

- forms cocoon made of silk and bits of debris to stay hidden
- can stay in cocoon for days or even months

FLYING WITH THEIR LEGS!

Adult fleas don't have wings, but they have very strong legs they use for jumping. In fact, some people say fleas can fly with their legs. Fleas can jump **distances** up to 200 times the length of their body.

How are fleas able to jump so far? They have pads where their legs are joined to their body. The **energy** stored in these pads is then used by their legs when they jump. It's like having springs for legs!

FREAKY FACT!

FLEAS CAN JUMP UP TO 3 INCHES (7.6 CM) INTO THE AIR.

A flea's ability to jump allows it to move from one host to another in search of more food.

FLEABITES

Fleas have to bite into the skin of animals and people to drink their blood. When fleas bite people, they leave red marks behind. The marks can be very **itchy**. Sometimes, the marks can turn into raised bumps on the skin. Fleabites show the places on an animal or a person where a flea had a meal of fresh blood.

People's bodies can get used to being bitten by fleas. When that happens, fleabites feel less itchy each time a person gets new bites.

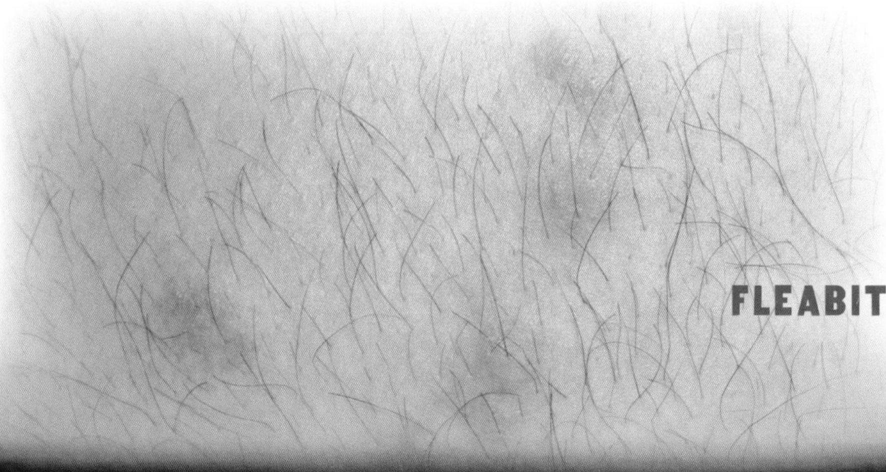

FLEABITES

This flea's body is filled with human blood.

THE BLACK PLAGUE

When fleas bite people, they sometimes leave behind more than just red bumps. They can leave behind scary sicknesses, such as bubonic plague. This sickness killed more than a quarter of the people living in Europe during the 14th century.

Fleas get bubonic plague by biting rats that are sick with it. Fleas then pass the sickness to humans by biting them. Bubonic plague is less deadly now because there are medicines to treat it.

FREAKY FACT!

BUBONIC PLAGUE CAUSES PEOPLE TO HAVE HEADACHES AND A **FEVER**. THANKFULLY, IT'S NOT SEEN VERY OFTEN IN THE UNITED STATES.

Bubonic plague killed millions of people in European towns, such as the one shown here. It was often called the "black plague" or "Black Death."

SPREADING OTHER SICKNESSES

Fleas can also spread a sickness called murine typhus to people. However, like bubonic plague, only a few people each year get sick with murine typhus in the United States. Those who do get it often have a fever and body aches. Murine typhus goes away with medicine, though.

Murine typhus also comes from sick rats and mice. Fleas bite these sick animals, and then they bite people, passing the sickness on to them.

FREAKY FACT!

FLEAS CAN ALSO HAVE PARASITES. WORMS AND OTHER TINY LIVING THINGS CAN MAKE A HOME INSIDE THE BODY OF A FLEA.

Oriental rat fleas, such as the one shown here, are the most common carriers of murine typhus among flea species.

FINDING FLEAS

How can people get rid of fleas? It's important to look for flea eggs, larvae, and cocoons near places where host animals live and sleep. Adult fleas are found on the bodies of their hosts.

Using a vacuum is a great way to get rid of fleas because it sucks up fleas at every stage of their life cycle. Flea combs can be used to find and remove fleas on animals. Special dusts, sprays, or dips can also be used to kill adult fleas on a host animal.

FLEA COMB

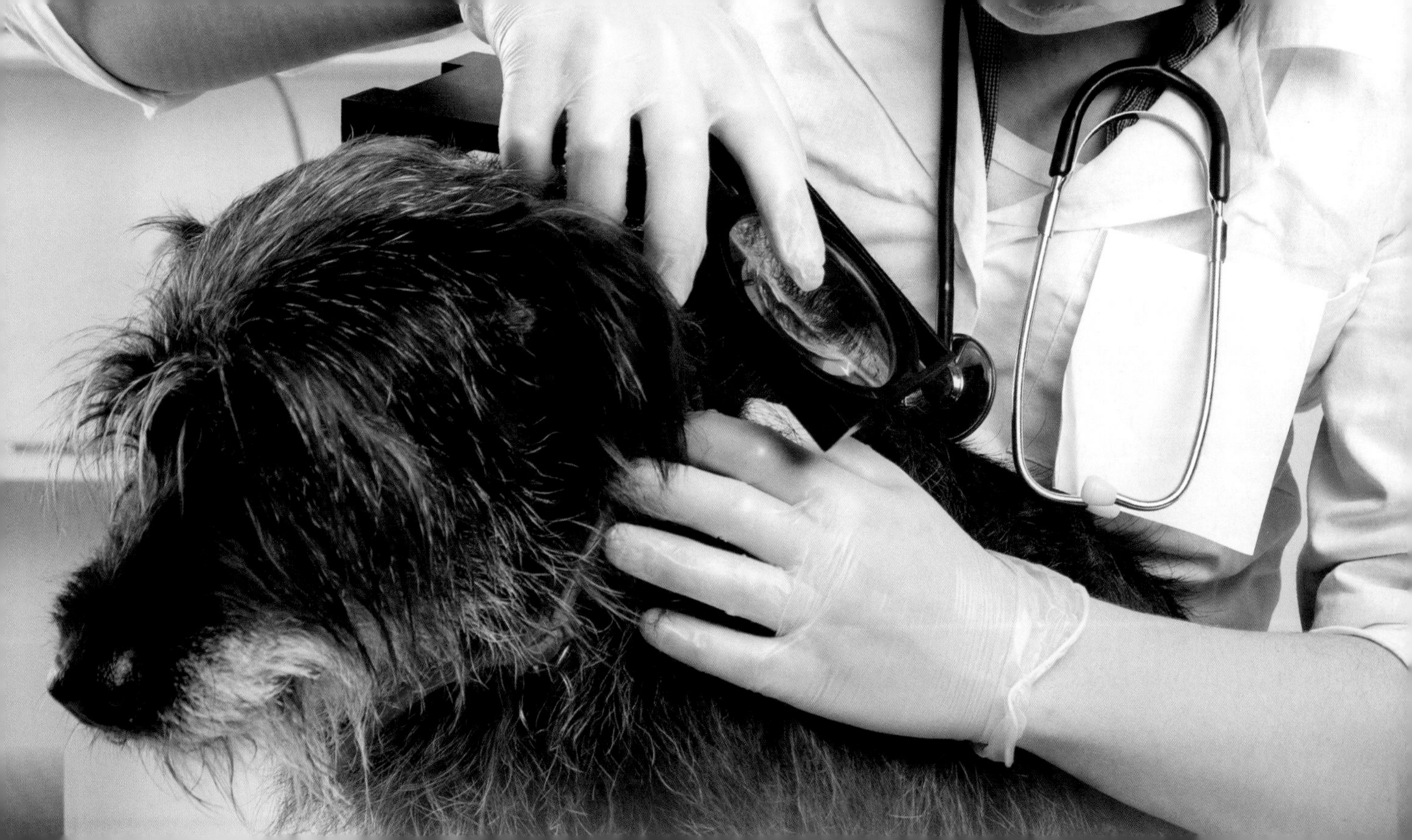

big problem for people, too! They can leap from host to host, drinking as much blood as their body can hold. After they're done drinking, they can leave an itchy reminder of their meal behind.

Fleas have brought about the deaths of millions of people by spreading sicknesses. While those sicknesses aren't as deadly today, fleas are still creatures no one wants to find in their house or on their body.

GLOSSARY

adaptation: A change in a living thing that helps it live better in its habitat.

distance: The space between two points.

energy: The power or ability to make something work.

fever: A rise above a person's usual body temperature.

itchy: Producing an unpleasant feeling on your skin that makes you want to scratch.

mammal: Any warm-blooded animal whose babies drink milk and whose body is covered with hair or fur.

spine: A long, sharp part of a plant or animal.

stage: A step in the growth of a living thing.

INDEX

WEBSITES

Due to the changing nature of Internet links, PowerKids Press has developed an online list of websites related to the subject of this book. This site is updated regularly. Please use this link to access the list: www.powerkidslinks.com/bfp/flea